Psycholinguistics

Table of Contents

I- An introduction to psycholinguistics

Psycholinguistics is the study of the mental phases of language and speech. It is essentially concerned with the ways in which language is represented and processed in the brain. An interdisciplinary branch that encompasses both linguistics and psychology, psycholinguistics has been tremendously impacted by the field of cognitive science in general.

Simply defined, it is the study of the relationship between human language and human mind (Maftoon and Shakouri, 2012). In research, three important processes are investigated in psycholinguistics: (1) language production, (2) language comprehension, and (3) language acquisition.

From many questions that psycholinguistics tries to solve, it, precisely, addresses two questions (1) what knowledge of language is needed for us to utilize language? and (2) what cognitive processes are involved in the normal use of language?

In recent years, psycholinguistics has developed rapidly and expanded into several sub-disciplines as cited in Chaer (2015) below:

A.   Theoretical psycholinguistics. It focused on theories of language relating to human mental processes in language, such as phonetics, diction, syntax design, discourse, and intonation.

B.   Developmental psycholinguistics. It is related to language acquisition, both first language acquisition (L1) and second language acquisition (L2). It examines phonological, semantic, and syntactic acquisition, process in stages, gradually, and integrated.

C.   Social psycholinguistics related to the social aspects of language, including social identity.

D.   Educational psycholinguistics discussed general aspects of formal education at school, including the role of language in teaching reading teaching proficiency, and improving language ability to express thoughts and feelings.

E.   Neuro-psycholinguistics focused on the relationship between language, language production, and the human brain. Neurology experts have managed to analyze the biological structure of the brain and analyzed what happens with the input language and how language output programmed and set up in the brain.

F.   Experimental psycholinguistics included and experimented in the whole range of language productions and activities, language behavior, and result.

G.   Applied psycholinguistics is concerned with the application of the outcomes of six sub-disciplines of psycholinguistics clarified before in specific areas that require it, covering psychology, linguistics, language learning, neurology, psychiatry, communications, and literature.

Terminology

The term psycholinguistics was introduced by American psychologist Jacob Robert Kantor in his 1936 book, "An Objective Psychology of Grammar." The term was popularized by one of Kantor's students, Nicholas Henry Pronko, in a 1946 article "Language and Psycholinguistics: A Review." The emergence of psycholinguistics as an academic discipline is generally linked to an influential seminar at Cornell University in 1951.

"Psycholinguistics is the study of the mental mechanisms that make it possible for people to use language. It is a scientific discipline whose goal is a coherent theory of the way in which language is produced and understood," says Alan Garnham in his book, "Psycholinguistics: Central Topics."

According to David Carrol in "Psychology of Language," "At its heart, psycholinguistic work consists of two questions. One is, What knowledge of language is needed for us to use language? In a sense, we must know a language to use it, but we are not always fully aware of this knowledge....

The other primary psycholinguistic question is, what cognitive processes are involved in the ordinary use of language?

By 'ordinary use of language,' is meant such things as understanding a lecture, reading a book, writing a letter, and holding a conversation. By 'cognitive processes,' is meant processes such as perception, memory, and thinking. Although we do few things as often or as easily as speaking and listening, we will find that considerable cognitive processing is going on during those activities."

From a pedagogical perspective, in his definition of speaking for instance, Bygate (2010:1-9) differentiates between knowledge that is the know how or the required amount of language grammar and vocabulary, and the skill which refers to a series of related processes during speech production like making decisions rapidly, adapting what we say to the actual situation, and adjusting our conversations as unexpected problems arise.

He also refers to Wilkins' distinction between motor-perceptive skills (p. 5) namely perceiving, recalling, and articulating and considers this aspect of speaking as the superficial one or the context-free one, and interaction skills where the learner moves from a language learning situation to a language using situation. In fact, Bygates refers to these as being at the same time motor-perceptive and interaction skills since they involve the ability to use language in order to satisfy particular demands. This is why psycholinguistics is considered interdisciplinary and is studied in different fields such as psychology, cognitive science and linguistics.

In the first place, psycholinguistics that means psychology of language is the study of the psychological and neurological factors that empower humans to learn, use, grasp and produce language ("Altman", 2001, p.1).

Due basically to a lack of cohesive information on how human brain works, recent research makes use of biology (natural science concerned with the study of life and living organism), neuroscience (t h e scientific study of how information concerning faculties such as perception, language, reasoning , and emotion is represented and transformed in a human or other animal nervous system or machinery, linguistics and information theory(a branch of applied mathematics and electrical engineering involving the quantification of information.)

To study how brain processes language, there are a number of sub- disciplines with non-invasive techniques for studying the neurological workings of the brain, for example neurolinguistics has become a field in its own right. Psycholinguistics covers the cognitive processes that make it possible to generate grammatical and meaningful sentences out of vocabulary and grammatical structure as well as the processes that make it possible to understand utterances, words, texts, etc. (Miller & Emas , 1983) .

A Short Historical Excursus

The original use of the word "psycholinguistics" was in J.R Kantor Objective Psychology of Grammar (1936), in which Kantor as an ardent behaviorist attended to reject the idea that 1 language reflected any form of intended cognition or mind . According to Kantor the German psycholinguists tradition was simply wrong .The term more firmly established with the publication in 1954 of a report of a working group on the relationship between linguistic and psychology entitled psycholinguistics.

The studies of relationship between behavior and cognitive characteristic of those who use language seem to be the origin of Psycholinguistics. Wilhelm Maximilian Wundt a German physician, physiologist, philosopher, and professor, in the 19th century derived psychology from biology and called himself psychologist. The term psycholinguistics was coined in 1936 by Jaco

Robert Kantor in his book An Objective Psychology of Grammar and started being used among his team at Indiana University but its use finally became frequent thanks to the 1946 article "Language and psycholinguistics: a review", by his student Nicholas Henry Pronko. It was used for the first time to talk about an interdisciplinary science "that could be coherent" as well as in the title of Psycholinguistics: A survey of theory and research problems, a 1954 book by Charles E Osgood and Thomas A. Sebeok.

What does Psycholinguistics explore exactly?
Psycholinguistics explores the relationship between the human mind and language. It treats the language user as an individual rather than a representative of a society - but an individual whose linguistic performance is determined by the strengths and limitations of the mental apparatus which we all share. Its agenda is to trace similar patterns of linguistic behaviour across large groups of individual speakers of a particular language or of all

languages. In this way, we hope to attain insights into the method in which the configuration of the human mind forms communication - although the processes involved may be so well established that we are no longer conscious of hem.

In fact, the notion that language is a product of the human mind gives rise to two interconnected goals, both the concern of psycholinguistics:

a)   to establish an understanding of the processes which underlie the system we call language.

b)   to examine language as a product of the human mind and thus as evidence of the way in which human beings organize their thoughts and impose patterns upon their experiences.

Psycholinguistic research falls into six major areas, some of which overlap:

Language processing

What exactly happens when we are listening, speaking, reading and writing? What steps or stages do we follow when engaging in these skills? How do we manage to change a grammatical structure into a piece of information?

Language storage and access

How is vocabulary stored in our mind? How do we manage to find it when we need it? What form do grammar rules take?

Comprehension theory

How do we manage to bring world knowledge to bear upon new data that is introduced to us? How do we manage to make a global meaning representation from words that we hear or read?

Language and the brain

What neurological activity corresponds to reading or listening? Where does the brain store linguistic knowledge and semantic concepts? What neurological and muscular activity is involved in speech? Can differences in the human brain account for the fact that our species has developed language?

Language in exceptional circumstances

Why do some children grow up with language impairments such as dyslexia or stuttering? How does brain harm or affect language? What is the effect of deep deafness upon language acquisition?

First language acquisition

How do infants come to acquire their first language? What stages do they go through in developing syntax, vocabulary and phonology? What evidence is there that we possess an innate faculty for language which enables us to acquire our first language, despite the supposedly poor quality of the input we receive?

II- Brain structure and processes involved in language and psychology

LANGUAGE AND THE BRAIN

Three important issues emerge in relation to language and the brain.

Comparison

In what way do our brains differ from those of other primates which do not possess language?

Nativists argue that a human infant must have some kind of genetically transmitted language faculty in order to acquire language as rapidly and successfully as it does. If that is the case, then we can expect the human brain to be different in structure from those of primates not capable of language. Of course, evidence of differences between human brains and those of other species does not necessarily prove the nativist case. We might approach the issue from the opposite (cognitivist) angle and suggest that differences in the operation of the human brain are what enabled us to evolve language when other species could not.

Localisation

Where is language located in the brain?

Attempts to locate language in the brain have a long history. Added impetus was given to the issue when Noam Chomsky (1965) and others drew attention to the fact that every normal child successfully acquires a first language, no matter what its intelligence or learning style. This suggested to some commentators that language must be an independent faculty and not part of our general powers of thought and reason. Evidence supporting this hypothesis comes from accounts of individuals who have serious learning difficulties but in whom the language faculty appears to be spared. It is therefore of interest to find how language relates to the other operations performed by the brain.

Lateralisation

Is there a difference in the way the right side and left side of the brain contribute to language? At what age does that difference become established? Early evidence suggested that damage to the left side of the brain impaired language in a way that damage to the right did not. Where the damage occurred before the age of about five, the sufferer would sometimes fully recover their powers of speech. Hence a theory (Lenneberg, 1967) that, in infancy, the relationship between the two parts of the brain is flexible enough for language to relocate itself on the right when necessary. This led to much discussion as to whether the periods of flexibility constitutes a Critical Period for learning a first language, after which a child is not be able to achieve full competence.

The human brain

Medicine took many centuries to figure out that the brain is used for thinking and several more centuries to have some clues about how something the consistency of oatmeal could have anything to do with ideas, dreams, and feelings. In fact, this

"mind-body problem" is still a very hard question and the source of many discussions among psychologists, neuroscientists, linguists and philosophers. How could three pounds of cells, fat, and blood inside the hard shell of a skull make us human beings instead of robots? In this section, we consider only how our brains make it possible for us to use language to hear, speak, sign, read, write, and understand.

A quick geography of the brain

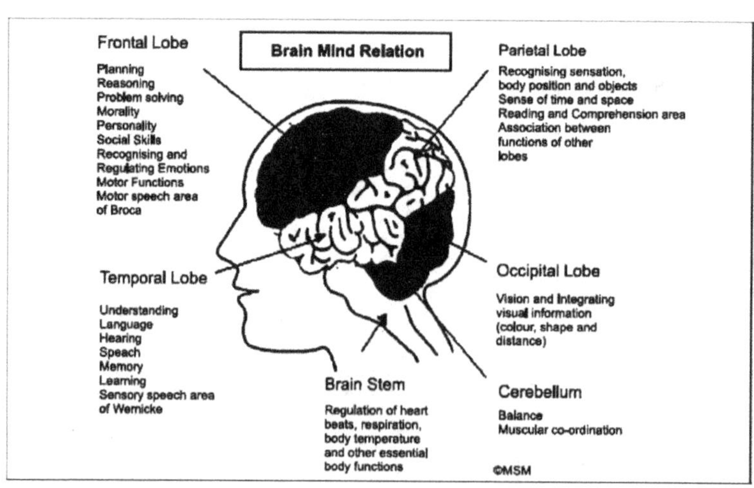

The general structure of the brain is that of a whole which is divided into vertical halves that seem to be mirror images of one another. It looks much like a walnut with the two parts joined around the middle, except that there is little space between the two halves in the real brain. Each half of the brain is called a hemisphere. There is a left hemisphere and a right hemisphere. The hemispheres come out of the brain stem, which connects to the spinal cord. The hemispheres maintain connection with one another through a bundle of fibres called the corpus callosum. The brain, together with the spinal cord, is referred to as the central nervous system of the human body. There is a covering on each hemisphere, called the cortex, which is a furrowed outer layer of cell matter. It is the cortex that is concerned with higher brain functions in both humans and animals.

The cerebral cortex advanced last in the course of evolution. While in fish, for example, the cerebral cortex is barely visible, and is one of the smallest parts of the brain, in humans it has increased in size and complication to become the biggest part of the brain. In time, due to the growth in the number and complexity of brain cells in the life of the human, the cerebral cortex becomes more dense and takes on a greyer and less pink appearance.

Each cerebral hemisphere is divided into four parts or lobes: from front to back there are the frontal, temporal, parietal (located above the temporal), and the occipital. This division of the brain into lobes is loosely based on physical features and not on actual separations.

General functions such as cognition (to some degree) occur in the frontal lobe, hearing occurs in the temporal lobe, general soma esthetic sensing (feeling in the arms, legs, face, etc.) in the parietal lobe, and vision in the occipital lobe. Each hemisphere has these lobes with these functions. As we shall see later, there are other hemispheric- specific functions that are also located in some of these areas. For example, the left hemisphere typically involves language.

The corpus callosum not only serves to connect the hemispheres but is itself a principal integrator and coordinator of the mental processes carried out in the two hemispheres.

Language areas:
The areas that have been proposed for the processing of speaking, listening, reading, writing, and singing are mainly located at or around the Sylvian and Rolando fissures. Several specific areas have been identified:

1-   The front part of the parietal lobe, along the fissure of Rolando, is primarily involved in the processing of sensation, and may be connected with the speech and auditory areas at a deeper level.

2-   The area in front of the fissure of Rolando is mainly involved in motor functioning, and is thus relevant to the study of speaking and writing.

3-   An area in the upper back part of the temporal lobe, extending upwards into the parietal lobe, plays a major part in the comprehension of speech. This is 'Wernicke's area'.

4-   In the upper part of the temporal lobe is the main area involved in auditory reception, known as 'Heschl's gyri', after the Austrian pathologist R. L. Heschl (1824–81).

5-   The lower back part of the frontal lobe is primarily involved in the encoding of speech. This is 'Broca's area'.

6-   Another area towards the back of the frontal lobe, 'Exner's centre', may be involved in the motor control of writing.

7-   Part of the left parietal region, close to Wernicke's area, is involved with the control of manual signing.

8-   The area at the back of the occipital lobe is used mainly for the processing of visual stimulae. Some of the neural pathways that are considered to be involved in the processing of spoken language:

A.   Speech production. The basic structure of the utterance is thought to be generated in Wernicke's area and is sent to Broca's area for encoding.

The motor programme is then passed on to the adjacent motor area, which governs the articulatory organs.

B.   Reading aloud. The written form is first received by the visual cortex,then transmitted via the angular gyrus to Wernicke's area, where it is believed to be associated with the auditory representation. The utterance structure is then sent on to Broca's area, as in (1).

C.   Speech comprehension. The signals arrive in the auditory cortex from the ear, and are transferred to the adjacent Wernicke's area, where they are interpreted.

Left and right hemispheres control opposite sides of the body

The brain controls the body by a division of labour, so to speak. The left hemisphere controls the right side of the body, including the right hand, the right arm, and the right side of the face, while the right hemisphere controls the left side of the body. Those who have suffered a cerebral haemorrhage, commonly called a 'stroke', provide clear examples of how this kind of cross-over control operates. A stroke in the right hemisphere of the brain will affect victims on the left side of the body. Thus, they can lose control over the muscles in the left hand, left leg, and the left side of the face (including that side of the tongue and mouth). A stroke to the left part of the brain will similarly affect the right side of the body.

Hemispheric dominance

Typically, the left hemisphere dominates the right. Now, even though the hemispheres of the brain divide the labours of the body, they do not do so evenly. In a sense, we might say that the body cannot serve two masters: one side must take charge. For a human to have the two hemispheres competing over which hand or foot should be used first to fight off an attacker or to jump at an animal in a hunt would not be advantageous for the survival of the species. This phenomenon, where one hemisphere is the controlling one, is called dominance.

Generally, animals, including chimps, have not been thought to have a genetic hand/foot preference. Rather, individual animals were thought to develop a personal preference over their lives. However, some recent research seems to indicate there may be left and right hemispheric differences in chimps and that such differences might result in preferences (Freeman et al., 2004). Clearly, though, such differences are not as striking as in humans.

Lateralized hemispheric functioning

Besides their general functioning, the hemispheres have some very specialized structures and functions. Some functions occur in one hemisphere while other functions occur in the other hemisphere. This separation of functions is called lateralization. Incoming experiences are directed to the left or right hemisphere depending on the nature of those experiences, be they speech, faces, or sensations of touch. We will see that speech production and speech understanding are mainly located in the left hemisphere.

Left-hemisphere specializations

Research has clearly shown that language centres predominate in one hemisphere or the other. The main language centres are Broca's area, in the front part of the brain, Wernicke's area, towards the back, and the angular gyrus, which is even further back. Broca's area and Wernicke's area are connected by tissue – the arcuate fasciculus. (See the figure below).

For most people, language is in the left hemisphere: for roughly 99 per cent of right- handers and about two-thirds of left-handers (Damasio and Damasio, 1992). Language is located in the right hemisphere in less than 5 per cent of the US population.

For these persons, in addition to language, all other specific left- and right-hemispheric functions are also reversed. For convenience sake, we shall use the majority case (left hemisphere for language, etc.)

for the purpose of discussion. In addition to language, the left hemisphere is concerned with logical and analytical operations, and higher mathematics.

Right-hemisphere specializations
The right hemisphere is involved in recognizing emotions, recognizing faces, and perceiving the structures of things globally without analysis. Unilateral right-hemisphere stroke can lead to problems with both immediate and delayed memory, when patients have trouble learning and remembering individual words (Halper and Cherney, 2004). If the area of the brain that deals with faces, for example, is damaged, the person will not be able to recognize the faces of people, even close family, and even that person's own face when looking into a mirror! Needless to say, such a situation is devastating to the life of the person. The right

hemisphere also deals with music and non-linguistic sounds, such as noises and animal sounds. Interestingly, patients with right hemisphere damage seem to have difficulties in processing pitch as a prosodic syntactic distinction. When presented with a sentence 'The queen said the knight was singing' (a man is singing) as opposed to 'The queen, [pause] said the knight, [pause] was singing' (a woman singing), a patient with the right-hemisphere damage was reported to have difficulty apprehending this syntactic distinction (Hoyte et al., 2004). However, new research shows that the right hemisphere has some language functions and can take over the complete language functioning of the left hemisphere when that hemisphere has been surgically removed or damaged.

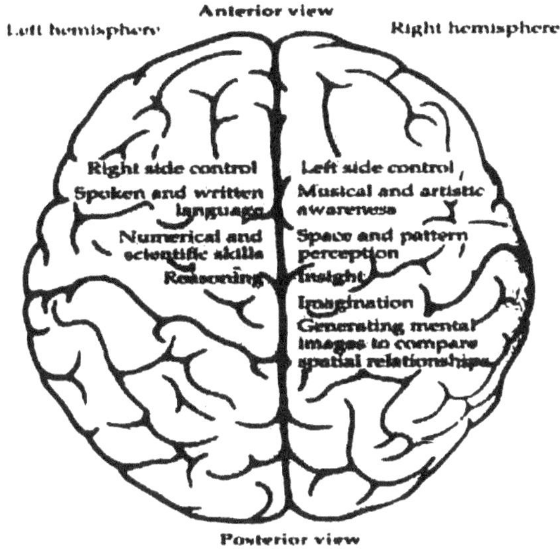

Lateralized hemispheric functioning

Split-brain effects

Certain aspects of lateralization have been dramatically confirmed by the work of Sperry (1982), who separated the two hemispheres of the brain by severing the connecting tissue, the corpus callosum, of a number of patients. Such a drastic operation was believed necessary to save the patients, who were suffering from extreme cases of epilepsy.

After surgery with the corpus callosum no longer intact, information no longer flowed from hemisphere to hemisphere as it does in normal persons. The functions of the complete brain were no longer integrated. Such being the case, it was possible for Sperry and his group of researchers to test some of the abilities of the separate hemispheres.

It was found that 'split-brain' persons could still use speech and writing in the disconnected left hemisphere but that their right hemisphere had little such capacity. In normal persons, the right hemisphere has more capability.

When tactile (touch) information passed to the left hemisphere, split-brain patients were completely capable of verbally describing objects and talking about things they had just touched. If, however, the touching experience of patients passed only to the right hemisphere, they could not talk about the experience at all; the information could not be passed through the corpus callosum to the left hemisphere for expression in speech because the corpus callosum had been severed.

The right hemisphere, in general, was also incapable of imagining the sound of a word, even a familiar one, and patients failed simple rhyming tests, such as determining by reading which word, 'pie' or 'key', rhymes with 'bee'. The right hemisphere was found to be good at spatial tasks such as matching things from their appearance, such as being able to correctly reassemble halves of photographs.

In August 2000, BBC News reported an interesting case of a man, who suffered from epilepsy and had to go through surgery, which separated the left and right hemispheres of his brain. Now the left brain performs well at language skills, while the right brain does best with shape puzzles (The Man With Two Brains, 2000).

Language areas and their functioning

Broca's area, the motor area, and speech production
Pierre Paul Broca was a French pathologist and neurosurgeon (1824–80) who made the first great discovery regarding brain and language. He discovered a

certain area of the cortex that is involved with the production of speech; that part of the cortex bears his name, Broca's area.

Broca further noted that the speech area is adjacent to the region of the motor cortex that controls the movement of the muscles of the articulators of speech: the tongue, lips, jaw, soft palate, vocal cords, etc. He posited that speech is formulated in Broca's area and then articulated via the motor area. Subsequent research substantiated Broca's theory. The link between Broca's area and the motor area was later shown to be the nerve fibres of the arcuate fasciculus. The speech-production process would begin in Broca's area, pass on through the arcuate fasciculus to the motor area and from there to the articulators of speech for vocalization.

Wernicke's area, the auditory area, and speech understanding
Speech comprehension Carl Wernicke, a German neurologist (1848–1905), in considering that Broca's

speech area was near the part of the brain that involves areas that control the articulators of speech, investigated whether two other areas of the brain are involved in the process of speech comprehension. In his research he discovered, near the part of the cortex in the temporal lobe that receives auditory stimuli, an area that was involved in the understanding of speech.

Wernicke hypothesized that this area, later named Wernicke's area, must in some way be connected to the auditory area. Later research showed that these areas are indeed connected, by fibres of the arcuate fasciculus.

The model that Wernicke posited over a century ago is still largely the model which most researchers use today in describing how we understand speech. According to Wernicke, on hearing a word, the sound of a word goes from the ear to the auditory area and then to Wernicke's area. It is from Broca's area that the vocalization of speech would then be activated.

Reading

When a word is read, according to Wernicke, the information goes from the eyes to the visual area of the cortex in the occipital lobe, from there to the angular gyrus, then to Wernicke's area and then to Broca's area, which causes the auditory form of the word to be activated. Wernicke had the mistaken belief that all written words had somehow to be speech activated (said aloud).

Recent research in brain-scan imaging actually shows that the latter part of the reading process, where Wernicke thought that Broca's area would be activated, does not occur in many instances. In other words, one can directly recover the meaning of written words without having to access their sound. This must be the case, for example, in rapid reading where speed precludes any such distinctive activation.

Language in other areas and the other hemisphere

Although most language processes occur in Broca's area, Wernicke's area, and the angular gyrus, some language functioning occurs elsewhere in the left hemisphere, as well, and some even occurs in the right hemisphere. (Right-hemisphere language functions are a relatively recent discovery and these are considered in the next section.) The ability to understand the meaning of intonation, such as the rising tone of a question, the ability to interpret emotional intentions, such as anger or sarcasm, from inflections In the voice, and the ability to appreciate social meanings from something such as whispering, may very well be located outside of what have been traditionally regarded as the main language areas of the brain.

Say, the cerebellum and basal ganglia used to be considered as subcortical nuclear systems dedicated to the regulation of motor function, the cerebellum being in charge of the real-time fine-tuning of movement, and the basal ganglia, the selection or inhibition of action commands. However, contemporary neuroimaging studies have revealed that the cerebellum is actively involved in search strategies for verbal responses, and the basal ganglia appear to participate in the selection of specific lexical items (Murdoch et al., 2004).

However, the exact way in which these processes regulate linguistic function remains largely undetermined.

Right-hemisphere language abilities

Typical language functions

While the left hemisphere is involved in most language tasks, recent evidence indicates that the right hemisphere too is involved in language processing (see Beeman and Chiarello, 1998, for a good review). More precisely, 'both hemispheres receive similar input and both attempt to process input, for every language process.' In addition, 'the hemispheres compute information differently at each level of processing (e.g. semantic processing), so that each hemisphere is most adept at handling particular inputs and producing particular outputs' (Chiarello & Beeman, 1998, p. x).

Understanding discourse and other minds

There is increasing evidence that the right hemisphere is critical for understanding discourse (Hough, 1990; Kaplan et al., 1990; Beeman, 1993, 1998; Brownell and Martino, 1998; Stemmer and Joanette, 1998; Paradis, 2003). Thus, patients with right- hemisphere damage have impairments concerning narrative script, interpretation, integration of information or conceptualization of the unit as a whole, construction of new conceptual models, and inferences about another person's beliefs and intentions (Stemmer and Joannett, 1998).

The right hemisphere has an ability to use 'knowledge of the world', involved in scripting, where a number of sentences are related to a topic. Patients who have damage in their right hemisphere show structuring problems in story recall (Moya et al., 1986), and their speech is disrupted, particularly at the level of discourse, jumping from one topic to another incoherently (Brownell and Martino, 1998).

The right hemisphere can take over left-hemisphere functions

It is significant to remember that the brain functions as a whole. Any task is represented by a network of areas. For the brain's overall performance the amount of removed tissue matters more than its location (Posner, 2001). Therefore, the brain is able to readjust its circuits to process language in case normal processing cannot occur. For example, brain scans revealed that blind persons receive verbal communication help from the brain areas that normally process visual and touch information in sighted people (Ariniello, 2000). Researchers at the University of Marburg in Germany compared language processing time in blind and sighted subjects who were asked to decide if the last word made sense in sentences like 'we sleep in a tent when we go camping' as opposed to 'tomorrow Bobby will be ten years hill'. They found out that blind persons were twice as fast on the task. This difference in timing can lead to the idea that the part of the brain normally associated with vision is redirected to process language by blind people (Jones, 2000).

Brain plasticity accounts for the growing evidence that damage to language areas in the left hemisphere of young children is compensated for, with the right hemisphere taking over the reacquisition of language. This sometimes happens with adults, as well. Recently, MRI scans of stroke patients revealed that about six months after the stroke, the area on the right side of the brain corresponding to the inferior frontal gyrus was heavily used to restore language skills. It suggests that the brain develops previously underused areas and transfers language processing to those areas to help compensate the damage (Rosen et al., 2000). While the extent of functional plasticity is not yet established, it is clear that the right hemisphere is capable of taking over left-hemisphere functions.

The bilingual brain

Recent neurolinguistic research has shown growing interest in how bilinguals represent different languages in the brain. Two central issues have been the focus of research: whether different languages are represented in the different hemispheres of the brain, and if the age at which a second language is learned is related to lateralization. As we shall see, results are not consistent on either question.

Studies showing right-hemisphere involvement

Albert and Obler (1978), Karanth and Rangmani (1988), and Wuillemin et al. (1994) mentioned greater contribution of the right hemisphere in bilinguals than in monolinguals. Albert and Obler (1978) argue that 'the right hemisphere plays a major role in the learning of a second language, even in adulthood' (p. 243). Their position is based partly on the finding that aphasia (language dysfunction) is more likely to be found following righthemisphere lesions in bilinguals (10 per cent) than in monolinguals (1– 2 per cent). If the right hemisphere is damaged, and aphasia results, then they argue that the location of the second language must be in the right hemisphere. Indeed, there is evidence of different degrees of recovery after a stroke for each language (Paradis, 1977, 2004; Junque et al., 1995). Extreme cases have shown impairment for one language postoperatively, with spontaneous recovery after eight months (Paradis and Goldblum, 1989). A more recent case has been used to suggest that there is a clear neuroanatomical dissociation between the languages (Gomez-Tortosa et al., 1995).

Studies finding no dominance

A number of studies, on the other hand, have reported no difference in lateral dominance for the first and the second language. For example, Soares (1982, 1984), Walters and Zatorre (1978), and Zatorre (1989) found no difference between bilinguals and monolinguals. Galloway and Scarcella (1982), in a Spanish–English dichotic-listening study, found no evidence for the right hemisphere being involved more in the initial stages of informal, adult, second-language acquisition.

In sum, while findings are not consistent, the fact that right-hemisphere difficulties are involved in so many studies suggests the distinct possibility that a second language sometimes locates in the right hemisphere and sometimes not. There may be variables that determine hemispheric location but these have not been identified as yet. One such factor may be the age at which the second language was learned.

Sign language
Left-hemisphere damage affects signing Right-handed deaf signers, like hearing persons, exhibit aphasia when critical left-hemisphere areas are damaged (Poizner et al., 1989). Approximately one dozen case studies provide sufficient detail to implicate left-hemisphere

structures in sign-language disturbances. A subset of cases provide neuroradiological or autopsy reports to confirm left-hemisphere involvement, and provide compelling language assessment to implicate aphasic language disturbance. In addition, there are five cases of signers with right-hemisphere pathology.

Since their sign-language skills were relatively intact, this would indicate that the left hemisphere is the primary location of sign language.

Disruptions in sign-language ability following left-hemisphere damage are similar to those patterns found in hearing users of spoken languages. For example, execution of speech-articulation movements in hearing persons involves the cortical zone encompassing the lower posterior portion of the left frontal lobe (Goodglass, 1993), which is the same region implicated in sign-language production (Poizner et al., 1987).

Language impairments following strokes in deaf signers exhibit the characteristic pattern of left frontal damage leading to non-fluent output with spared comprehension, while left posterior lesions yield fluent output with impaired language comprehension. These impairments are local in nature, and do not reflect general problems in symbolic conceptualization or motor behaviour.

Therefore, the left hemisphere appears to be centrally involved in sign language, as it is with non-signers. The right hemisphere also is intricately involved with signers but in ways different from that of non-signers.

Other Important Processes involved in Language and psychology

Memory

Human beings are born with a complex, interrelated system for categorizing and storing every event experienced throughout life. Audio, visual, sensory, and emotional information is integrated, yielding images that are linked to lexical items as events. These are stored in memory.

Memory refers to the processes that are used to acquire, store, retain, and later retrieve information. There are three major processes involved in memory: encoding, storage, and retrieval.

Not all information is equally easy to recall, since different types of events are stored in different parts of memory, based on significance.

The most current and widely accepted model of memory consists of three general stages: sensory (events that are experienced in real time), short term (which holds a limited amount of information for a limited time period), and long term (which stores events and is composed of layers of levels, based on the nature of the input. As an event is experienced, neurons are fired, encoded, and stored in the area of the brain responsible for the corresponding type of information. During a memory search (lexical retrieval), encoded neurons are activated in order to reconstruct the past event. Lexical retrieval and discourse comprehension are highly dependent upon both short-term and long-term memory. Studies in memory give insight into:

- Lexical storage and retrieval

- Categorization of lexical items

- Pathways of retrieval

Levels of Memory

Sensory memory (SM) involves the storage of sensory 'events', those that are perceived by any of the five senses in real time. SM is the shortest type of memory, such that sensory information may only be retained for .2 to .5 of a second, since it is quickly replaced by subsequent input. Furthermore, SM has no rehearsal component so stimuli cannot be stored.

Unless intentionally ignored, sensory information is processed automatically. This is why we sometimes experience 'sensory overload'. This occurs when our senses are bombarded with too much incoming sensory information. Instead of processing everything, we either select what we want to experience, or abandon the source of the overload and shut out all perceptions.

When our senses receive a manageable amount of stimuli, one of three processes can occur. SM can deliberately disregard information such that it disappears, or perceive information, at which point it will either decay (be quickly forgotten). Perceived information that receives attention or focus will move on to short- term memory.

Visual stimuli are processed by the iconic memory, aural by echoic memory, and touch by haptic memory. Memory associated with taste is processed by the 'taste' cortex, whereas smell or odor memory seems to be in a class of its own. This storage of this type of stimuli are processed by the olfactory bulb and olfactory cortex, which are very close to areas of the brain involved in memory. This most likely accounts for why we remember smells so vividly, and why certain odors remind us of places, people, and experiences.

Short-Term Memory

Information in SM that receives our attention is moved along to short-term memory (STM). STM holds information recently processed, for relatively immediate use and is limited in terms of the amount of information it can store at any given time. Its job is primarily to keep information active and readily accessible.

In other words, STM can be described as a finite amount of temporary, limited storage space where sounds and words are held while sentence processing takes place. So, when you are listening to a sentence, you need to 'store' the first few words while you process the rest.

This is also where information is stored during any learning process. Initial information, i.e., such how to draw a syntax tree, must be stored so that subsequent material, i.e., the components of a noun phrase, can be related back to earlier input. This is why some students take notes. Since STM holds a limited amount of information, new stimuli will replace the older such that one forgets what was said 5 minutes previously.

Miller (1956) showed that humans can remember 5-9 chunks of information at a time. STM is used up more quickly if the processing system is doing too many tasks at once, or if one overly demanding task is being performed, like trying to memorize a lengthy list of items. STM does not store complete concepts, but holds the most important information readily available. In the event that this is not needed immediately, the stimuli will move to long-term memory.

Working Memory
Working memory (WM) is the fundamental component of STM, so much so, that these two terms are often used interchangeably. WM is often referred to as the 'search engine' of the brain. It is characterized by four crucial components. WM operates over a matter of seconds, it

provides temporary storage for incoming stimuli, it is the holding place for information that receives the most focus, or attention, and it is the component of the brain where information is manipulated.

Long-Term Memory

Long-Term Memory (LTM) holds unlimited amounts of information indeterminately. Even though no one can remember every minute detail of every moment throughout a lifetime, it is generally believed that LTM stores all meaningful episodic events, i.e., those that have received adequate attention, have been sufficiently rehearsed, and have been attributed semantic properties.

So why do you not remember what you ate for breakfast December 20 of 2002? Even though LTM is good at integrating and synthesizing information, it is less able to keep smaller bits of information distinct from each other. Recall of any given event is based on its perceived importance and rehearsal.

So, while you may not remember your breakfast on a non-descript day, you are more apt to remember that which you consumed on a special holiday (importance). An individual who learns a foreign language as a child, however does not try use it until adulthood, will struggle to remember that which s/he learned. Yet, as soon as a certain amount of studying (rehearsal) occurs, this language competence is restored, or remembered.

The retrieval of information stored in LTM involves incorporating real-world knowledge, from which inferences are drawn and connections are made, again, based on semantic relationships.

There are two main storage components in LTM:

Explicit memory is conscious awareness of facts and events (Declarative Memory).

•   Episodic Memory: the ability to recall personal experiences and events as images; details about past experiences.

- Semantic Memory: the ability to recall personal experiences and events that are meaningful in terms of connections between sources of recurring information which has been learned

Implicit Memory is unconscious and holds procedural information.

- Procedural Memory: the ability to remember strategies in task performance as sequential events or as sets of stimulus-responses.

Perception

The concept of perception is very complex. It is deeply rooted in cognition (Merikle and Joordens, 1992, 1997), psychology (Vecera & O'Reilly, 1998; Peterson, A. & Rhodes.G, 2003) and philosophy (Kleiman, 2003; Crane, 2011). It can be affected by physiological influences such as age and fatigue or social, cultural and communication influences as it can be impacted by attributions and self-concepts and these might be clarified in either simple or complex methods.

The Thesaurus Dictionary, for instance, attributes the following definition to perception "the act or faculty of apprehending by means of the senses or of the mind; cognition; understanding or an immediate or intuitive recognition or appreciation", while Encyclopedia Britannica defines it as "the process whereby sensory stimulation is translated into organized experience".

From a psychoanalysis viewpoint, experience or percept, is the co- constructed and multiform outcome of the stimulation and understanding of a whole process based on the faculty of association. That is why perception is believed to be influenced by many factors like unconscious ideas, learning, expectations, needs, values, past experiences, relations and conflicts.

In theoretical research based on psychoanalysis, the similarities, relations or conflicts found between various types of stimulation and their associated percepts suggest inferences that can be made about the properties and characteristics of the perceptual process.

On the other hand, from a practical and pedagogical perspective, the perceptual process cannot be directly checked and measured except by the perceiver who is responsible for classifying, comprehending, and organizing the selected data. Therefore, the validity of any perceptual process can be checked only in an indirect way. To this end, the utility of scientific research lies in the fact that perceptions that are derived from theory will then be compared with corresponding statistically checked empirical data to find out similarities, conflicts, new associations and discrepancies. This is why studies and scientific empirical data about perception are very pertinent to understanding crucial details in psycholinguistics.

Automaticity Automaticity is a process believed by a number of researchers to play a major role in L2 learning particularly when dealing with spoken skills. According to Mclaughlin as reported by Gass (1997:148) "automaticity has to do with a learner's response which has been built up through the consistent mapping of the same pattern of activation over many trials". This means that routines that are practiced and repeated by learners in class do help them to gain automaticity.

Bygates (2009:23) defines routines as 'conventional ways of presenting information'. He talks about frequently recurring types of information structures which help learners acquire the habit of speaking and these can be either information routines like narration, description, and instruction or interactional routines like interview situations, conversations at parties, radio or television interviews. This also leads to a relatable controversial issue of how these 'frequently recurring types of information structures' can facilitate speaking.

III- Theories Underpinning Psycholinguistics Role of the linguistic theories

Historically, traditional grammarians have focused their study of language on the written mode which, according to their belief, constitutes 'the language' as opposed to speaking which is a 'corrupted form' of the official language. Celce- Murcia (1991:3) registers how very few learned scholars mostly churchmen, philosophers and politicians used to produce highly eloquent speech at a time when it was very difficult for the public to handle speaking. The result on language teaching has been concern on the written form at the basis of the spoken form.

With the emergence of modern linguistics, however, the spoken form of language has acquired a new status based on a number of considerations. For example, speaking is the primary means of communication used by all members of language communities. Not all languages of the world are written, while all are spoken. Also since the first function of language is communication, all spoken languages are equally important (Saussure, Bloomfield). For these reasons, it is the form that has been the subject of enquiry by modern linguists.

American structural Linguists, for example, at the early decades of the 20th century sought to document languages spoken by indigenous people. They relied on observation to infer the rules and patterns of those languages. For the same reason, a strong focus on oral language was developed.

One of the main principles of structural linguistics, for example, is that language is speech not writing (Bloomfield, 1933, Fries, 1945, 1961). This position, according to them, is not arbitrary since a child first learns how to speak and it is only after the development of his sensory-motor skills that he starts to learn how to write.

Structuralists, therefore, adhere to the belief that speech is the original or primordial form of language, and that writing is its derivative form. The underlying assumption maintains that 'speech' is 'primary' or the 'real thing' and that 'writing' is 'secondary' or its 'representation' (Kern and Jean Marie, 2005: 382).

On the other hand, language study within the structural framework was concerned with the formal aspects of spoken language with an aim of discovering the regular patterns and structures. The focus of linguistic enquiry was thus the structure of language not its functions. For instance Saussurean belief that "la langue est une forme et non une substance" tremondousely impacted the field of linguistics. His theory of the syllable, and his concern with Latin and Greek phonology fall within the same backdrop. Bloomfield was inspired greatly by Saussure since American linguists laid more emphasis on spoken languages too and on synchronic descriptions taking into account that the languages of aborigines in America did not have written codes.

This emphasis on the formal mode has predominated and shaped famous linguistic trends especially after the introduction of Saussure's semiology science. In structuralist terms, sign is a complex entity of two distinct elements 'a signifier' and 'a signified' (Eugenio Donato,

1967:550).The idea here is that structures represent a shift from a surface code of language to an infrastructure layer of meaning and the discovery of this meaning proceeds not by general axioms but rather by the systems

 governing those relations (William Free, 1974:66). The argument of whether the signifier holds any presupposed kinship to the signified or that the relationship between them is arbitrary has mapped the route of thought in structural linguistics.

As an illustration, some of the key Saussurean notions of opposition in language "in which one element only acquires or signals meaning in contradistinction to some other element with which it contrasts" (Kronenefeld and Decker, 1979:512) have largely influenced structural linguistics. It could be argued that emphasis on the formal analysis of language, and its dwelling on the relations among structures impacted language teaching too.

Before closing this brief discussion of structural linguistics, it is worth mentioning that American structural linguistics adopted the same principles as behavioral psychology in discarding mental processes in the study of Language.

In reaction to structural linguistics (and behavioral psychology), Chomsky's theory of linguistics initiated a revolution in the fields of both linguistics and psychology. Chomsky rejected the view of language as verbal behaviour or as a set of habits and maintained that language is a mental process acquired through children's mental ability to infer the rules from the input they are exposed to (1959, 1965, 1975).

For him, the domain of inquiry of linguistic theory is "competence", the implicit and ideal linguistic knowledge that makes it possible for speakers to produce and understand an infinite number of sentences based on a finite set of rules, and not performance, the actual use of language (Chomsky, 1965). He advocates that understanding

 competence is crucial to understanding the nature of actual performance. In his theory, the sentence is the main unit of investigation to understand grammar.

One should mention, however, that even though Chomsky's theory is also based on the study of the structure of language (mainly syntactic structure), he is concerned with the internal/mental structures underlying language use. His linguistic theory proposed an account of the underlying structure of language and people's knowledge of their language. This theory along with cognitive psychology opened up new perspectives for language learning theories and pedagogy.

Role of psychological schools
The impact of psychological schools on language study and language learning came as a reaction to the criticism addressed to linguistic theory for its emphasis on the linguistic structure and the formal analysis of language,

and its dwelling on the relations among structures. The need to go beyond linguistic description thus marked the shift of interest to psychological theories which contributed to the development of language learning theories.

The next section will be devoted to a review of the role of psychological schools. Two major schools will be discussed below namely behavioural and cognitive psychological schools given their close relationship with structural and cognitive linguistics and psycholinguistics especially in their treatment of human language, and given their impact on approaches and methods of language comprehension and particularly the speaking skill.

The impact of psychological schools on language study and language learning came as a reaction to the criticism addressed to linguistic theory for its emphasis on the linguistic structure and the formal analysis of language, and its dwelling on the relations among structures. The need to go beyond linguistic description and observation helped to promote psychological theories which presented an extension and a development of language learning theories. Therefore, the next section will be devoted to the role of the psychological schools.

Two major schools will be discussed below namely behavioural and cognitive psychological schools given their close relationship with structural and cognitive linguistics respectively in their treatment of human language, and given their impact on approaches / methods to language in general and language learning and teaching in particular.

Behavioural psychology
The father of American behaviourism, Watson (1913) views psychology as an experimental branch of natural science. For him, the field of study of psychology is the external behaviour of human beings not their mental states (e.g. consciousness) which cannot be studied

objectively. He advocated that thought is nothing more than internal speech.

Skinner, another American behaviourist, is known for his study of human language through this famous article "Verbal behaviour" (1957) in which he advocates that language learning is not different from learning any other behaviour like walking, chewing, etc. It is verbal behaviour children learn through practice and repetition. The principles of Skinner's theory combined with principles of structural linguistics had a great impact on language learning / teaching and led to the emergence of teaching approaches which favoured the spoken language in L2 classes.

Later on, cognitive psychologists have challenged the limitations of behaviorism especially its focus on observable behavior. Therefore, a mental view to language has been developed with the introduction of cognitive psychology where the incorporation of mental structures in the learning processes paved the way for more profound reconsideration to L1 (first language) and L2 (second language) acquisition.

Innateness Theory

Noam Chomsky's innateness theory (or nativity theory) proposes that children have an inborn or innate faculty for language acquisition that is biologically determined. It seems that the human species has evolved a brain whose neural circuits contain linguistic information at birth and this natural predisposition to learn language is triggered by hearing speech. The child's brain is then able to interpret what she or he hears according to the underlying principles or structure it already contains.

IV-   The importance of Cognitive psychology

What Is Cognitive Psychology?

Cognitive psychology involves the study of internal mental processes—all of the things that go on inside your brain, including perception, thinking, memory, attention, language, problem-solving, and learning. While it is a relatively young branch of psychology, it has quickly grown to become one of the most popular subfields.

There are numerous practical applications for this cognitive research, such as providing help coping with memory disorders, increasing decision- making accuracy, finding ways to help people recover from brain injury, treating learning disorders, and structuring educational curricula to enhance learning.

Learning more about how people think and process information not only helps researchers gain a deeper understanding of how the human brain works, but it allows psychologists to develop new ways of helping people deal with psychological difficulties.

For example, by recognizing that attention is both a selective and limited resource, psychologists are able to come up with solutions that make it easier for people with attentional difficulties to improve their focus and concentration.

Findings from cognitive psychology have also improved our understanding of how people form, store, and recall memories. By knowing more about how these processes work, psychologists can develop new ways of helping people improve their memories and combat potential memory problems.

For example, psychologists have found that while short-term memory is quite short and limited (lasting just 20 to 30 seconds and capable of holding between five and nine items), rehearsal strategies can improve the chances that information will be transferred to long-term memory, which is much more stable and durable.

The cognitive school and speech production
Cognitive psychology has opened up new perspectives for the study of the learning process in general including L1 acquisition but also L2 acquisition which has benefited from research methods used in L1.

Piagetian work on child psychology, for instance, has paved the way for great processes underpinning language acquisition from infancy to adulthood. Siann (1989:74) studies how Piaget has outlined a developmental approach whereby humans use assimilation and accommodation principles to process information in a mental organized structure. These mental organized structures are prior conditions to any speech production or discourse operation.

According to Funt (1971), in his study of Piaget and structuralism, mental or logical processes have been the major advocacy of Piaget who has always believed in the impact of cognition and mental logic on the learning process. In this respect, Funt (1971:17) states that:

Piaget sees logical procedures as equivalent to or rather as growing out of natural processes and consequently as pre-linguistic or pre-discursive…

logical functions are seen by Piaget in terms of operations, which are ultimately sensory- motor operations …

Undoubtedly enough, Piagetian insight into human psychology has yielded profound reconsideration to the cognitive processes employed in speech production which is analyzed as comprising a number of operations underlying any speech entity.

From a psycholinguistic perspective, more recent psycholinguists have identified several processing components of speech production. Levelt (1994:91) , produces one of the greatest examples where he advocates that speaking contains at least three processes (1) intentions and thoughts, (2) items and sentences, and (3) sound production or articulation. These three levels of processing have their own properties speed of operation. He has designed a working model of the main cognitive processing components that cooperate in the production of fluent speech as shown below.

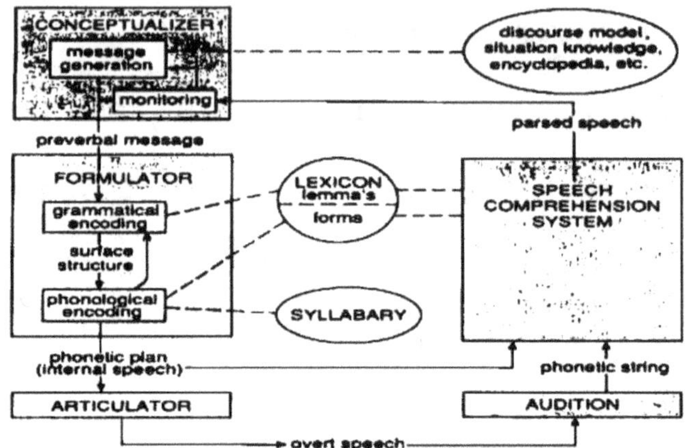

FIG. 5.1 Blueprint of the speaker. Boxes represent processing components; circle and ellipses represent knowledge stores.

Fig 1 (Reprinted with permission of the author, Willem Levelt)

Levelt explains how the blueprint of the speaker englobes the main processing components that are put in motion while producing fluent speaking. The slow strategic component is called conceptualizer, and as is the case with speaking functions, in trying to use speaking functions communicatively (e.g., to share a piece of information, or to make the interlocutor perform a certain action..etc), the speaker must select information that will reveal his message, and regardless of the nature of this message, it has to be cast in a linguistic form called here the formulator which achieves two main tasks namely: a-grammatical encoding: mainly choosing the appropriate words from the lexicon, and putting them in a corresponding syntactic order. This developing syntactic structure is a surface structure. In addition, there is b- phonological encoding: consists in generating an articulatory or phonetic shape for all words, and for the utterance as a whole.

The result is an articulatory plan where the utterances are specified, and this phonetic or articulary plan is what constitutes internal speech which is made producible through the human articulatory system or apparatus of breathing and food ingestion which Levelt describes as:

The most astonishing feats of evolution that is developed through our most complex and species-specific motor system, the carrier of a language. In speaking, more than a hundred muscles are coordinated to create the highly overlapping articulatory gestures that produce intelligible speech."(Levelt, 2009: 92).

Levelt explains that just as speakers manage to make speech operating from its intentional phase to its overt utterance or wording phase, and since speakers are their own hearers, they might come up with errors during delivery and might want to make use of self-repair and here the mediating processing component is the language comprehension system. Through the blueprint operating speech systems, we can see the considerable variables that interfere during a speaking situation.

But this view remains reductive since in addition to the linguistic patterns that speakers use, there are also functions speakers seek to fulfill in the real world. With the establishment of this new conceptual processing of speaking that aims at making speech operate from its intentional to its overt meaning however, there is a growing need to decipher what speaking rules or functions make of speaking an operative means to comprehend and interact with the exterior world and be part of a social group. A close investigation of what speaking ethnography is may provide answers to such a query. This will be searched for within the general framework of pragmatic and sociolinguistic theory.

V-   Psycholinguistics and language learning/teaching

In relation to language teaching, developmental psycholinguistics and applied psycholinguistics play significant roles in formulating effective ways of teaching. Psycholinguistics theory covered the language development of humans, in accordance with humans' physical and mental development. These theories are considered in designing language teaching programs and materials in order to be effective for the second language learners master the target language.

Harras and Andika (2009) mention three kinds of language teaching methods which are developed according to psycholinguistics principles: natural method, total physical response method, and suggestopedia method.

Basing on behavioral and cognitive psychology , audiolingualism and cognitive –code learning approaches to language teaching and communicative approaches are also recognized to be very impactful.

Approach and Method

Harmer (2001) offers distinct definition of these two concepts. Approach refers to theories about the nature of language and language learning serving as the source of practices and principles in language teaching. An approach describes how language is used and how its constituent parts interlock – in other words it gives a model of language competence. An approach describes how people acquire their knowledge of the language and make statements about the conditions which will promote successful language learning. A method is the principal realization of an approach. The originators of a method have arrived at decisions about types of activities, roles of teachers and learners, the kinds of material which will be helpful, and some model of syllabus organization.

Methods include various procedures and techniques as part of their standard fare.

Therefore, psycholinguistics has been used widely as fundamental theory in developing language teaching method. Some methods which were developed based on psycholinguistic approach are described as following (Harras and Andika, 2009)

Natural Method
This method is developed by Tracy D. Terrel. This method adheres to the fact that language learning is a reproduction of the way humans naturally acquire their native language. This method rejects earlier methods.

Psycholinguistic principles in language learning according this method are as following. a. Language mastery relies on learning language skills in natural context and less on conscious learning of grammatical rules. b. Learning a language is an effort to develop communicative competence, the ability to understand the speech of native speakers and native speakers understand the learners' speech without any error which can interfere with meaning.

c. Comprehension is primary than production. d. The model that underlies this method is five monitors theory: (1) acquisitionlearning hypothesis, (2) natural order hypothesis, (3) monitor hypothesis, (4) feedback hypothesis, (5) affective filter hypothesis.

The consistency of this method is shown by natural technique developed by teacher. Teacher stimulates the learners to competence activity such as problem solving, game, and humanistic affective. Problem solving is designed to train learners to find out a right situational answer or solution. Games are considered as an interlude activity, but it is designed to improve students' language competence. Humanistic affective is designed to implicate opinions, feelings, ideas, and reaction to language learning activity.

Total Physical Response Method

This method is developed by psychologist from San Jose State College, United States, James J. Asher (1966). Psycholinguistic principles in language learning according to this method are as following. a. Language competence will improve significantly by involving kinesthetic sensory system in language learning. This related to the fact that children are given utterances that require them to move physically. b. Comprehension is primary rather than speech production. Students are directed to achieve comprehension competences before they try to speak or write.

Related to kinesthetic theory, it is believed that there is a positive correlation between physical movements and students' language achievement. It becomes the focus in designing and applying appropriate language teaching technique in a certain topic. A spacious classroom is required in applying this method. The class ideally consists of 20-25 students. This method can be applied to teach children or adults. Grammatical rules are presented in imperative sentences because basically all materials are presented in imperative sentences. In this method, dictionary is unneeded because the meaning of words will be expressed by physical activities. Students usually do not get homework because language learning is performed together in the classroom.

Suggestopedia

This method is developed by Georgy Lazanov, a psychiatrist in Bulgaria in 1975. Psycholinguistic principles in language learning according this method are as following. 1. Humans can be directed to do something by giving them a relaxed atmosphere and opened and peaceful mind. These will stimulate nerves to easily respond and store the information for longer. 2. Before the lesson started, students are persuaded to relax their body and mind in order to gather hypermnestic ability, it is an incredible supermemory. 3. The classroom is set up with dim light, comfortable seats, relaxed atmosphere and classical music. 4. Laboratorial program and strict grammar exercise are rejected in the class. 5. Generally, material is presented in a long dialogue.

The characteristics of the dialogue are: (a) emphasizes vocabularies and content, (b) related to the real life, (c) practical utility, (d) relevant emotionally, and (e) some words are underlined and given the phonetic transcription. Each meeting in this method is divided into three time allocations. The first is reviewing the previous topic through discussion, games, sketch, or role playing. If students do some mistakes, teacher corrects it carefully to keep a positive atmosphere. The second is distributing the dialogue traditionally. The third is relaxing students. This is divided into two: active activity and passive activity.

Other impactful approaches to language learning/teaching:

Audiolingualism

Founded essentially on structural linguistics, especially Bloomfield (1933) and behavioral psychology (Skinner, 1957), audiolingualism is one of the most important approaches to language teaching which advocates the primacy of speech in the language classroom. Among its major tenets "Language is speaking not writing", "Language is set of habits", and "Language is Verbal behavior". In this regard, Skinner (1957:5) states:

What happens when a man speaks or responds to speech is clearly a question of human behavior and hence a question to be answered with the concepts and techniques of psychology as an experimental science of behavior.

Skinner thus advocated that, like all other behaviors, language is learned through repetition and reinforcement (positive or negative). Adhering to notions such as stimulus-response and operant conditioning, a behaviorist, quite expectedly, might consider effective language behavior to be the production of correct responses to stimuli. If a particular response is reinforced, it then becomes habitual or conditioned. Brown (1994:17) considers this to highlight the 'immediately perceptible aspects of linguistic behavior, the publicly observable responses and the relationships or associations between those responses and events in the world surrounding them'.

The idea that has characterized behaviorism- that observable behavior is perpetuated if reinforced- has affected language classroom. Therefore, teachers used to rely on reinforcement or positive feedback presumably used as a result of the ultimate success on the part of the learners having showed total grasp of a certain pattern.

In this regard, Williams and Burden (1997:10) in explaining how behaviourism has largely influenced language teachers, noted that within the audiolingual approach framework, much analysis had been done to consider the role of the learners who should be positive respondents to teachers' stimuli using such mechanisms as repetition and substitution. Blair (1991:24), on the other hand, clarifies how from an audiolingual perspective, language was considered as:

A definable set of structures with lexical exponents, which could be learned inductively, pattern by pattern, by means of a rigorously planned and carefully executed program of instruction based on the laws of conditioning and reinforcement.

Thus, audiolinguists advocate a considerable control over learners' oral production. A great effort is deployed to manipulate learners' errors in such a way that structural or grammatical correctness is the ultimate motive during the learning process. Thus, learning how to speak a language is seen as acquiring a set of mechanical habits or as Gass (2008:49) puts it "learning a language involved imitation as the primary mechanism, the language that surrounded learners was of crucial importance as the source for imitation".

In this way, behaviorist psychology along with principles drawn from structural linguistics shaped language teaching and directed it towards a mode of teaching advocating the supremacy of speech over writing, form over function and accuracy over fluency. This reductive perception has been criticized for the inactive engagement of learners both at the level of negotiation which lacks in this mode of teaching between the teacher and the learner and between learners themselves, as well as at the level of the passivity of the learner whose mission does not transgress mere responding or consumption of the structural patterns according to sequential or repetitive steps.

Cognitive-code learning approach
Based on both Chomsky's TGG (transformational-generative grammar) (Kyle, 2004) and Gestalt theory(Green, 2000), a cognitive psychological school, the

cognitive-code approach was critical of both GTM (Grammar Translation Method) and ALM (Audio Lingual Method).The first one because of its neglect of the spoken skill and the second for its emphasis on behavioral techniques such as repetition, drilling, memorization, etc. This approach, proposed between the 1960s and 1970s by Carroll (1966) and Chastain (1970), advocated that language learning involved active mental processes, and that it was not just a process of habit formation (as assumed by the ALM).

Thus language classes were still concerned with grammatical structures, but teaching/learning was based on understanding and meaning, hence the importance of meaningful practice. Lessons consisted in presenting examples of the target structures to make students understand the grammatical rule before practicing it in meaningful contexts. Teachers elicited dialogues which contained examples of the target structure, encouraging thus students' speaking through the elicited dialogues

The Communicative approach to Language Teaching (CLT)

A number of factors led to the emergence of the communicative approach to language teaching. Such factors include developments in the fields of sociolinguistics, pragmatics, philosophy of language, communication theory (Hymes, 1966, 1972; Austin, 1961, 1962; Searle, 1969, 1979), the work of applied linguists around the eighties, both British and American to name but a few: Wilkins (1974), Halliday (1976), Widdowson (1983), Van Ek and Alexander (1980), Littlewood (1981), Savignon (1983), etc.) who were discontented with the theories and methods of teaching prevailing in language classrooms before the appearance of CLT, as well as historical factors (e.g. the Council of Europe interest in promoting new language teaching approaches that help European citizens learn the major languages of the European community more effectively). Under these different influences, awareness was raised that language, above all, functions as a system of communication among social groups, and therefore, language teaching /learning should focus on the communicative functions of language.

Wilkins (1972), on the other hand, proposed a functional or communicative definition of language that could serve as a basis for developing communicative syllabuses for language teaching. Adopting the same view, Van Ek and Alexander (1980) designed a functional- notional syllabus for language classrooms which consists of notions (meanings) and functions (communicative acts). This syllabus was based on an analysis of learners' social communicative needs and was proposed as an alternative to syllabi based on linguistic items similarly to Wilkins' proposal of marking a shift from grammatically based to communicatively/functionally oriented syllabi.

Littlewood (1981) proposed procedures and practical activities for the teaching of language skills including speaking that promoted the use of language at the service of communication.

Psycholinguistics Approach and the Four Language Skills

Psycholinguistics theories have explained the mental processes that occur in human brain during a person produces and perceives a language. Language perception includes the activity of listening and reading, while the language production includes the activity of speaking and writing. The four activities are called as the four of language skills. Following will be described some benefits of psycholinguistics theories in language learning and teaching as explained by Demirezen (2004)

Psycholinguistics Approach and Listening Skill

Psycholinguistics researchers have indicated that in teaching listening, the intrinsic and extrinsic difficulties should be overcome in order to reach to a highly qualified listening activity. Intrinsic difficulty refers to the speed of the speech, number of unknown words, and prior knowledge about topic. Extrinsic difficulty refers to students' interest, motivation, purpose of listening activity, and noise in the environment. Psycholinguistics knowledge will help teacher to reduce the intrinsic and extrinsic difficulties. Teacher can prepare a listening text with topic that is familiar for students, consisting of 100 words, and including 10 new vocabulary items. Teacher also minds about the reading speed and the noise of

 environment. Moreover, teacher can increase students' interest and motivation by designing an interesting and comfortable class.

Psycholinguistics Approach and Reading Skill

Psycholinguistics approach resorts to text-based approach as a case of bottom-up processing so as to emphasize the comprehension activity and top- dawn processing to stress the fact that comprehension rests primarily on students' knowledge base. Bottom-up processing happens when someone tries to understand language by looking at individual meanings or grammatical characteristics of the most basic units of the text and moves from these to trying to understand the whole text. Top-down processing of language happens when someone uses background information to predict the meaning of language they are going to read to. Rather than relying first on the actual words, they develop expectations about what they will read, and confirm or reject these as they read. This theory emphasizes that the understanding the meaning of a text essentially rests on the prior knowledge of students. Psycholinguistics helps learners to reduce the intrinsic difficulties in reading activity by arousing the interest of the students onto the reading text. Teachers need to provide authentic and contextual reading material because if students are not properly exposed to authentic materials they may fail in seeing their relevance to the real world.

Psycholinguistics Approach and Writing Skill

Psycholinguistics helps in understanding the students' mistakes in writing. It has a clear contribution on spelling mistakes since in English words are not spelled as they sound. There is a hardship on this case because storing of the spelling of words and retrieve them on demand is very difficult.

Psycholinguistics approach indicates that there are mistakes in writing caused by agraphia, which must be treated properly. Psycholinguistics helps to find interesting topic to write. It serves to decrease the level of the difficulties in writing. It helps to specify the writing levels and writing types. It pins down the mechanic mistakes on punctuation and suggests certain cures for them.

Psycholinguistics Approach and Speaking Skill

Psycholinguistic approach has a workable control over the field of teaching speaking as a skill. It has specified several difficulties on speaking such as students' oriented difficulty. Psycholinguistics also explains that personality, like introvert and extrovert students, affects students' performance in language learning. Speaking defects like voice disorders, stuttering, and disarticulation are also psychological in origin caused by personality factor. There are also some traumatic disorders such as aphasia and autism caused by localized in damage. It is recommend therapies and counseling practices for such difficulties. Thus, the investigations of psycholinguistic approach have provided solutions for almost each type of language learning difficulty. With the knowledge, teachers can apply the appropriate techniques to teach speaking skills by considering the condition of the learner and find interesting topics to be discussed in speaking class.

BIBLIOGRAPHY

Altmann T. M. Gerry (2001), Psycholinguistics in review British Journal of Psychology 129–170 printed in Great Britain the British Psychological Society

Austin, J.L. (1962). How to do things with words. Massachussetts: Harvard University Press.

Austin,J.L. (1961). Philosophical papers. London: Oxford University Press.

Blair, R.W. (1991). 'Innovative approaches'. In Celce-Murcia (ed), Teaching English as a second language or Foreign language, Boston : Heinle and Heinle Publishers: 23-45.

Bloomfield,L. (1933). Language. London: George Allen & Unwin LTD

Burden,R.L & Williams.M. (1997). Psychology for language teachers: a social constructivist approach.Cambridge: Cambridge University Press

Bygate, Martin (2009) 'Teaching and testing speaking'. In Blackwell. W (ed), The Handbook of Language Teaching, Chichester: Blackwell Handbooks in Linguistics: 412-440.

Carroll, David. Psychology of Language. 5th ed., Thomson, 2008.

Carroll, J. (1966). 'The contributions of psychological theory and educational research to teaching of foreign languages'. In A. Valdman (ed), Trends in Language Teaching, New York: McGraw- Hill : 93-106

Celce-Murcia, M. (1991). 'Language teaching approaches : an overview'. In Celce-Murcia (ed) teaching English as a second language or as a foreign language, Boston : Heinle and Heinle Publishers: 3-10

Chaer, A. (2015). Psikolinguistik: Kajian Teori. Jakarta: PT Rineka Cipta

Chomsky,N. (1965). Aspects of the theory of syntax. Massachussets: The Massachusetts Institute of Technology

Chomsky,N. (1975). Syntactic structures. Berlin: Walter de Gruyter GmbH & Co. KG

Crane, Tim. (2011).'The Problem of Perception'. In Edward N. Zalta (ed.), The Stanford Encyclopedia of Philosophy.   Retrieved March 12,   2010   from <http://plato.stanford.edu/archives/spr2011/entries/perception-problem/

Demirezen, M. (2004). Relation between Psycholinguistic Approach and Foreign Language Learning and Teaching. Ondokuz Mayis Universitesi Fakultesi Dergisi, 17, 26-36.

Donato, E. (1967). 'Of structuralism and literature'. JSTOR, 82(5): 549-574. Retrieved December 25, 2009 from: www.jstor.org

Encyclopedia Britannica Retrieved From : https://www.britannica.com/ Fernández, E. M., & Cairns, H. S. (2010). Fundamentals of psycholinguistics. John Wiley & Sons.

Field, J. (2003). Psycholinguistics: A resource book for students. Psychology Press.

Field, John. Psycholinguistics: A Resource Book for Students. Routledge, 2003.

Funt,D. (1971). 'Piaget and structuralism'. JSTOR, 12: 15-20. Retrieved December 25,2009 from: www.jstor.org

Garnham, Alan. Psycholinguistics: Central Topics. Methuen, 1985.

Halliday, M.A.K., and R. Hasan. (1976). Cohesion in English. London: Longman Handbooks for Language Teachers. Oxford university press.

 Harmer, J. (2001). The Practice of English Language Teaching. Third Edition. London: Longman. Harras, K. A., & Bachari, A. D. (2009). Dasar-dasar Psikolinguistik. Bandung: Universitas Pendidikan Bandung Press.

https://www.linguisticsnetwork.com/psycholinguistics-an-introduction-to- memory-2/ Hymes, D. (1972).'On Communicative Competence'.

In J. Pride and J. Holmes (eds), Sociolinguistics: selected Readings, Harmondsworth: Penguin

Joordens, S., & Merikle, P. M. (1992). 'False recognition and perception without awareness'. Memory & Cognition, 20 : 151–159.

Kantor, Jacob Robert. An Objective Psychology of Grammar. Indiana University, 1936.

Khameis, M. (2007). 'Using creative strategies to promote students' speaking skills'. Retrieved April 2009 from marifa.hct.ac.ae at @EbookBrowse

Kleiman, Lowell .(2003).Review of "The Problem of Perception". Essays in Philosophy, Vol. 4: Iss. 2, Article 8.

Kronenfeld,D & Decker,H.W. (1979). 'Structuralism'. JSTOR, 8: 503-541. Retrieved December 25, 2009 from: www.jstor.org

Levelt, W. (2013). History of Psycholinguistics: The pre-Chomskyan Era. Oxford Scholarship online. Retrieved

Levelt, W. J. M. (1994). 'The skill of speaking'. In P. Bertelson, P. Eelen, & G. d'Ydewalle (eds), International perspectives on psychological science, Hove: Erlbaum: 89-103.

Lightbown, P. M., & Spada, N. (2013). How languages are learned 4th edition-Oxford

Maftoon, P., & Shakouri, N. (2012). Psycholinguistic Approach to Second Language Acquisition. The International Journal of Language Learning and Applied Linguistics World (IJLLALW. Vol 1 (1); 1-9 ISSN: 5389-2100

Merikle, P. M., & Joordens, S. (1997). 'Measuring unconscious influences'. In J. D. Cohen & J. W. Schooler (Eds.), Scientific approaches to consciousness, Mahwah, NJ: Erlbaum : 109-123.

Norita Purba. (2018) . Psycholinguistics in Language Learning and Teaching .Tell Journal, Volume 6, Number 1, ISSN : 2338-8927 47

O'Grady, William, et al., Contemporary Linguistics: An Introduction. 4th ed., Bedford/St. Martin's, 2001.

Peterson,A. & Rhodes.G, (2003). 'Analytic and holistic processing- The view through different lenses'. In Peterson, A and Rhodes, G. (eds), Perception of faces, objects, and scenes, New York: Oxford University Press.

Pronko, Nicholas Henry. "Language and Psycholinguistics: A Review." Psychological Bulletin, vol. 43, May 1946, pp. 189-239.

Pulvermüller, Friedmann. "Word Processing in the Brain as Revealed by Neurophysiological Imaging." The Oxford Handbook of Psycholinguistics. Edited by M. Gareth Gaskell. Oxford University Press, 2007.

Savignon, S. J. (1983). Communicative competence: theory and classroom practice. texts and contexts in second language learning. Reading, MA: Addison-Wesley

Searle, J. (1969). Speech acts: An essay in the philosophy of language. Cambridge, England: Cambridge University

Searle, J. (1979). Expression and meaning: Studies in the theory of speech acts. Cambridge: Cambridge University.

Siann, G. and Ugwuegbu, D.C.E. (1989). Educational psychology in a Changing World. UK, Cambridge: Cambridge University Press.

Skinner,B.F. 1957. Verbal Behavior. New Jersey: Prentice- hall Inc.

Steinberg, D. D., & Sciarini, N. V. (2013). An introduction to psycholinguistics. Routledge.

The free Dictionnary By Farlex. Retrieved January 17, 2010 from <ahref="http://www.thefreedictionary.com/perception">perception</a>

Vecera, S.P, & O'Reilly, R (1998). 'Figure-ground organization and object recognition processes: an interactive account'. Journal of experimental psychology. Human Perception and performance, 24(2): 441-462

Watson, J. B. (1913). 'Psychology as the behaviorist views it'. Psychological Review, 20 : 158-177

Wilkins,D.A. (1974). Second language learning and teaching. London: Edward Arnold.